The contents and creations herein are the property
of their respective artist(s) and may not be
used or reproduced without explicit written
consent. The following works have been donated
from prisoners across the United States and are
published with permission in order to amplify
the voices of queer and trans people surviving
imprisonment.

A.B.O. Comix Collective is sustianed by
volunteers, community donations, grant funding,
and various daring bank heists. We run on the
perserverance, bravery, kindness, empathy, and
love that our contributors share with us.

Edited by Ollie Mills
Cover Illustration by Feather
©A.B.O. Comix 2024

Table of Contents

Foreword

the other day a letter from you left
its home at the bottom of my bag and
found a new one in my heart-nest; bereft
of softness and the tools of rest, it spanned
the distance between my chest and my throat.
lodging there, it wound too tightly behind
my tongue, a spring coiled. its unbidden note
echoes throughout my body, unconfined
and home. i wouldn't swallow if i could.
strangers now know something of Your humor
through the rehomed tones of Your personhood,
the steel thresh of Your wit made consumer
of my host-heart flesh-nest, my pen your pen,
writing freedom - love letters until then.

- Ollie Mills

Part 1

No use being a bell
Wouldn't know how to ring

Scary Movie | 3 concrete walls...

3 concrete walls and a set of bars
Are the only life I've known
Razor wire around a fence
Is as far as my vision goes
Viewing the sky outside a window
Are the only heights I obtain
Because there's no room to spread my wings
After clipping them with this cage
Scheduled T.V., yeah that's for me
And eating when I'm told
Who knows, just might be a good meal
That's if it isn't cold
And if I'm searching for peace of mind
With a quiet place to hide
I'd have better luck making a wish
And clicking my heels three times
I can't blame others for my actions
They are mine and mine alone
And because of that I've found myself
In a home without a home

Left to dreams of taking flight

The Rainbow Sheep | Taking Flight

Twenty years later, I make my escape
And venture past the caution tape.

The time has come to break the mold,
Allow the truth a chance to be told.

My broken wings have been repaired.
Wind at my back, no longer scared.

I'm free at last, the work is done,
But the inner war has not been won.

I'll find the strength to carry on,
The pain and fear are finally gone.

Tattoo | 300 2nds

The time you can take out of your day
To show someone that you care.

The time it would take you to go online
And set up the phone so we could talk
more.

The time it would take you to go to the
TDCJ.gov website
And find out how to set up video visits.

The time it would take
To set up an account
So you could send me pictures.

The time it would take to get
A piece of paper,
Write the words "I love you,"
Put it in the envelope,
Address and stamp it
And put it in the mailbox.

    If you have not realized it by now,
    300 seconds is five minutes.

                And if you don't have
                      five minutes
                          a day
                            for me
                              now,
    Why would I have five minutes for you?

  I wrote this in less than 300 seconds...

H. Lee | One of Those Days

Another one of those days
Nothin goin' right
Can't get into my book
No use trying to write
If I were a writer
I'd call it a block
If I were a car motor
I'd have a knock
No use being a bell
Wouldn't know how to ring
Might try bein' Bird
If I knew how to sing
Tired of listenin' to music
Stations just won't come in
Having a really bad day
Sure could use my friend
Havin' a letter to read
Everything'd be alright
Just one letter
To read tonight

Manny Baez | What I Been Threw

When I was a young boy,
I used to pretend I had tattoos
But really though,
They was black and blues
Everywhere I had a bruise

Before they would fade,
They would tatt me up brand new
No one really knows
What I been threw

Tryna escape out the house and
Pushed my brother out the window
But really though,
It didn't make no sense
I got chased home from school
And hopped every fence

Really this meant
I didn't belong nowhere
I loved my mom to death
But she didn't care

After she took me to
A hospital and disappeared
After a three-oh-two
This isn't fair

I couldn't share most of the
Thoughts I was thinking
I'm looking up to rock bottom
As I'm quicksand sinking

Honest I'm like Lincoln

Cutting up with a razor blade
Quickly but slowly
My life fades away

I'm dancing with the devil
And the demons like to play
I'm hearing voices in my head
Do you think I'm okay?

Eeyore | What is Love?

What is Love?

Something one can play with,
or is it something that can be true?
A toy for a kid to just throw around,
or a heart that can shatter like Glass?
A game that never ends until the
person does not want to live at all.

Once I did this with the word Love,
only to have this ALL happen to me.
So now all I want is what is true
And not a toy or game.
Something that makes you feel whole,
something that makes you complete.
That person that no matter what,
You want to die for if you're without.

That person you will wake up to and kiss
    no matter what,
Even with dragon breath in the early hours
    of the day.
The one with stinky feet or the one who
    farts in their sleep,
The one you can just call MINE no matter
What.
For true Love never dies because
All you want to do
Is take care of what it is you
Truly LOVE.

So if you ask me What Love is to me,
I'd tell you it can
come true.

Even for you
It just takes time
For the right person to realize
That no matter what they LOVE and MISS
You.

So may my Love
Come home to me finally,
So we can truly be
One at last.
That is what Love is.

The Rainbow Sheep | Daydreamer

Time is the killer
Of all dormant dreams
Harsh words to be spoken,
But that's how it seems.

Live in the now
Let your future take shape
And cherish the moments
Before they escape

Don't hold onto anger,
You must let it go
To allow yourself
To flourish and grow.

Get a grip on your feelings
Of sorrow and shame.
If you sulk in that shit
It'll drive you insane.

Take a moment to breathe,
That's the first step to heal.
Make a vow to allow
The emotions you feel.

Part 2

*What better way to learn
to live
Than to be stricken of
your freedom?*

Joanna Nixon | Have you something to say?

Have you something to say?

Better listen with my eyes and ears!

You mind making noise yourself?

My Eyes more, ears less, no mouth!

Can I Hear, touch, watch?

I'll Paint, only let the light and dark
    speak!

You'll avoid my clumsy, useless sounding
    mouth?

I want to listen more, speak only when
    asked to!

Will you try, not at me, talk to me?

Scary Movie | One Breath

One breath, one second
One heartbeat at a time
One minute, one hour
Then the next one in line
What follows next
Is a day passing by
Venturing into the night
Footsteps for the next sunrise

One breath, one second
One miracle at a time
Each heartbeat makes it
A blessing to be alive

The Rainbow Sheep | The Phoenix
(A Day After Coming Out)

Rising from the ashes, like a phoenix, I
    will soar
A newfound source of power that I've
    never known before.
The time has come to spread my wings and
    finally take flight.
The sky is clear, so it appears - there's
    not a cloud in sight.
I lost my sense of purpose, I couldn't find
    my way.
I fell apart and took to heart the hurtful
    things they'd say.
Although the path is challenging, I know
    I'll make it through.
It's just a shame that it took twenty
    years for me to do.

Non-violent inmates are housed with other
inmates so full of hate and anger that all
they want to do is fight everybody.

How do you call this "rehabilitation"?

Instead of starting treatment programs as
soon as inmates enter the system, they are
forced to wait for years to the point it
is too late for the treatment programs to
do any good anyway.

How do you call this "rehabilitation"?

Every year the legislature promises
inmates hopes of going home early, but
also gives the system loopholes to take
those hopes away.

How do you call this "rehabilitation"?

Instead of sending inmates to facilities
that are more specialized to meet their
medical and mental health needs, they are
sent to general population facilities that
practically shun those needs.

How do you call this "rehabilitation"?

Eric Perez | To Imprisonment

What better way to learn to live
Than to be stricken of your freedom?
I committed no crime -
Okay, that's a lie -
But how am I to recover
When given no reason,
No purpose to be something more?

But what luck, what fortune!
I do have a purpose, a reason:
To help my fellow chattel
Look beyond the cowl of apathy
To the day when they will be seen
As beasts no more.

Part 3

*is it
tragic to care too much*

David Snyder | Present, Right Now pt. 1

Myriad of thoughts
the Dharma has bequeathed
     tools
to settle
and scrutinize
this mind
there is nothing new
                    under the sun
I attempt to
             discriminate
to find the value of
             interconnected
             interdependent
phenomena
         to share
to Do No Harm
Liberate All Sentient Beings
yet
chattel
anathema
contrarian
tacitly alllowed corporate STATE
to deny me the honor as serving as
                  Voice to the Voiceless
is it
tragic to care too much

Scary Movie | Dying By Inches

How thick do the scars have to get
Before you start going numb
Until the pain is the existence
That's become the total of the sum
When you're no longer hanging on
To the thinnest of thinnest of threads
And you're not counting your life in years
But the shallowest of breaths.

When hope is no longer a life line
But the afterbirth of a thought
And dreams no longer inspire
Only remind you of what is lost
And what is that heartbeat you hear
Counting the seconds like a clock
Tick, tick, ticking towards its reckoning
An elegy the only cost.

When your hands are tied with your own
        tears
And there's not a damned thing you can do
Quiet desperation, bound and gagged
Screaming 'til your face is blue
When you keep searching for your shadow
Just to stare into the abyss
Accepting with arms wide open
Your demons in the darkness.

How far do you think
You would fall into its depths
Until the pleas you start moaning
Are invitations for Death
And you would agree to anything
As you slowly die by inches

Anything to stop the pain
The suffering seems endless.

The Rainbow Sheep | Silent Cries

My demons have resurfaced, it's far too
much to bear.

At times I feel I'm drowning and no one
seems to care.

A whirlpool of my wicked ways is
starting to emerge.

It's taking all my sanity to silence every
urge.

I never thought I'd feel this way, or shed
so many tears.

It's like I popped the cork on all my
deepest, darkest fears.

Most my life's been fight or flight, as sad
as that might seem.

I wish I could escape it all, take refuge
in my dreams.

All this pain inside my brain is messing
with my head.

I wish that I could sit and reminisce with
you instead.

You'll never know the weight of all the
sorrow in my soul.

The deal is done, the Devil's come to make me pay his toll.

If only things were different, I'd do everything I could.

To not be such an asshole with a fucked up childhood.

Save me from temptation, I've been down that road before.

And help me fight these monsters, I can't face them anymore.

My body's weak and tired, no longer have the power

To cast these demons out of me, my mind they will devour.

I can't control the anger and the overwhelming rage,

Like endless chapters in a book with a doom on every page.

A neverending story, a movie with no sequels.

I'm stuck here in a prison now where everyone's my equal.

The silent cries I held inside have turned to screams and shouts.

Emotions locked within a cage are making
their way out.

My head's above the water now, the shore
is now in sight

So, I'll just keep on swimming and I'll
pray I'll be alright.

H. Lee | Old Letters

Reading old letters
The pages worn and thin
Read once, twice, three times
Then read once again
Read so much, so often
Familiar words to memorize
Though the joy of each one
Still a pleasant surprise
Reading old letters
Pages worn and thin
Reading and hoping
One will come again

Scary Movie | Timeless Despair, pt. 2

How can you tell the difference
Between the damned and the divine
When all that separates them
Is a barely visible line
And the only difference
Is the purpose of intent
Resolution of one's deeds
And what your actions meant
When the best of intentions
Isn't the road paved in gold
But the path that leads to hell
Burdening a heavy soul
A timeless, timeless despair
Spent in your own afflicted hell
With every ember of regret
The pain that lights an oil well
Even knowing your demons
Does it make you their master
Does it make the pain hurt less
And the scars heal faster
Does it make the memories drift away
For you to forget
Zephyr winds carrying
The careworn images as forfeit
How can you tell the difference
Between the damned and the divine
When it's the same scale that weighs
The heart and soul and mind

Part 4

Sweet to simply... be

Scary Movie | Wonder

I wonder
if I could have ever really known
all the wonders of this world
before I met you girl

Now nothing
can equally compare
to the luminescent flare
of an ardent fire so rare

If you would've told me yesterday
the eight wonders would fade away
the moment that I saw your face
that your smile would replace

The wonders
of all I've ever known
of all the wonders of this world
the day I met you girl

Now nothing
can equally compare
to the luminescent flare
of your ardent fire so rare

H. Lee | Puppy Love

If I were a puppy
Could I follow you everywhere
Whimper at your feet
So you know I'm there
Would you pick me up
For a hug and a kiss
I'll slobber all over you
In true puppiness
Would you let me in your room
On guard where you sleep
Ever watchful over you
Hearing every peep
Could I go with you
For walks in the countryside
Man and beast best stand clear
When I'm at your side
I'd be your constant companion
A very faithful friend
All I ask is to be with you
And perhaps a scratch on the chin

Gary Farlow | Orchard of We

From blossoms we arrived
The promise of things to come
Nourished by ideals
Watered by words
Like a forest of strength
Our numbers are many
The colors of a rainbow
Bleeding into one voice
No longer willing to accept the status quo
The fruit of humanity ripened
Into a song for freedom and equality
Our fruit is not bitter but sweet
For we bear no grudge, only love
Sweet like the air a convict breathes
Walking out the prison gates
Sweet, like the first day of classes
At a university for one previously denied
Sweet to simply...be.

Summer Breeze | The Reason Why I Cry

Someone asked me a question:
Why do you cry?
Is it a show of grief
Or is it pure relief?

I answered:
Crying gives me freedom
Crying gives me peace

Crying cleansed my soul
It helped to make me whole
That's the reason why I cry.

If you are imprisoned
Living in a hopeless cell
It's okay to cry
It will help you escape your hell

Crying can make you happy
Crying can set you free
An unofficial out date
No more chains, cuffs, or misery.

Manny Baez | 30 to 60

I'm having suicidal thoughts
I hope they don't turn into actions
'Cause I don't want to
Give people the satisfaction
So if anyone is asking
I'm doing alright
But I'm slowly crashing
Like grandma walking on ice
'Cause 30 to 60
Sounds a lot more like life
So every single night in my cell I pray
'Cause where I am
You either a predator or prey
They are frauds
And you must believe me
These rats get a green sheet
They leaving
And these other people talk behind your
back deceiving
A hundred and twenty something more
seasons
Before parole sees me - and it's not even
guaranteed
That they're gonna tell me to pack it up
and leave
That's why I can't be at ease
Because free is a tease and she's a sleaze
Hard to recieve, like a letter or a
birthday card
I'm in a different world: Avatar
When I'm walking alone trapped
up in this yard
They say life is hard unless you make it
But when the shake-down comes

The guards strip you naked
And my psychiatrist fakes it
And acts like she cares
But she wears outfits so they stare
That's the only reason why they share
I'm a stand-up type of guy
I don't need no chair
So I guess I'm a square,
'Cause I live in a box
But the jack-in-the-box
Thinking outside the box
Yeah my bottle gonna pop
And I ain't talking about soda
My next cellie a mouse
In a cage with a cobra
So many times I told you
I need some mental support
'Cause Imma always fall short
Like my appeals to court.

Tsunami | Be Agitated

Do not fear agitation, for agitation is
part of the rhythm of life; put it in
motion, stir it up

Do not fear the movements that decenter
what you always thought permanent

You carry within the center of your
understanding the compass to show you the
way

Carry with you the love that will hold you

The vision that will guide you, the
relationships to all beings and the

World that will ground you. Go in peace
and in gentle motion, agitation to stir
this world to the side of love.

Tsunami | Se Agitador

No temas a la agitación pues tal vez el
Ritmo de la vida misma: ser puesto en
movimiento, incitarte.

No temas los movimientos que descentras
en lo que creías permanente.

Llevas dentro el centro de tu
entendimiento,
La brújula que te muestra el camino.

Lleva contigo el amor que te sostendrá,
las visiones que te quitarán, las
relaciones con todos los seres y el mundo
que te enraizan la tierra.

Ve en paz y con una suave agitácion mueve
A este mundo hacia el lado de amor.

Part 5

I only write when
I am lost.

Ms. Billie | Untitled

It was different from the womb
Already bound for the tomb
Mistreated from the start
And abused by the heart

Misunderstood for sure
Always seeking a cure
There's nothing wrong with me
Why won't they just let me be

Lonely but never alone
Forced my heart to stone
Set about seeking a friend
Thankfully I found you in
                              the end.

Nero & Sakura | My Heart

I try so damn hard
Not once remember my thoughts
Truth be told I can't
So I carve a place soon be forgot

Demons bite my skin
As your scorpion's tail stings my eyes
My fist buries my skin
Crying my eyes out who soon dies

Thinking how you used
A filthy toy like me not as a couple
Because how a gentle touch like mine
You throw me away as a pebble

Did you remember that night
I let you in as you grew in me
Now my soul can't breathe

Abandon my love and every time
I do see you it never happens

I still want to believe these words
because I'm torn, madly laughing

I will hate you for ripping my world,
my heart and everything

Hopefully I hear somebody saying a
Prayer to let their heart sing

Because my heart can't and I'm wishing
For this pain to go away

Though stuck on the very last step
My heart wants me to stay

But I don't want to, as love has
Changed my anger, tortured it to rage

As suicide clings to my lonely heart
And my last page

Baby Jae | Your World

When we step from our homes
Our jobs
Our cells

From our bikes
Our cars

From our phones
Our trails

The difference between us
Seems obvious and true

The meaning behind how you look at us
Versus the fairness in how we see you

Either from birth or just a decision
We chose to make in our lives

Through our joys of being free
Or through our laughter and high fives

We notice how people
Not only husbands and wives

Will stop, look, and stare
With eyes that despise

While we try to contrive
A way to simply live

An equal exchange would be fair
To receive all that we give

We bring to this world:
Culture! Not shade

Queer, gay, lesbian or transgender
Uniqueness openly displayed

The same sky you see
Trust! We see too

Oh, and these beautiful
Clouds? We also fly through

My sisters, my brothers,
Here is the realest truth

We don't just live or strive
We excel because that's

What we do.
It's our world, too.

Nero & Sakura | Apart

Humans are all pathetic, obsessed
The art of my style ruined, posessed
With this and that they only tend to bark
Hating others, running their mouths
People are torn apart.

At least I know others will get a turn
To read what I wrote. Any poem I write
You can do with as you please
It's just wasted space
To keep holding onto those feelings.

I only write when I am lost.

Gary Farlow | Why I Write

I am old now;
I have no progeny
to carry on my name.

My writings are my children
nurtured in the womb of my mind,
given birth in ink on pristine paper,
sired to go forth in the world
like footprints in the sands of time.

My words will leave a legacy
to say that I was here.

The writings, like benign spirits,
will walk the earth long after me.

Why is it that an artist
is never truly appreciated
until they are long in the grave?

Perhaps my words will kindle
the musings of some aspiring writer,
encourage another to breathe life on paper
and continue along the path
of Whitman, Frost, Poe,
and me.

H. Lee | A Book

Bars do not a prison make
If one has a book to read
Stone and steel seem to disappear
Simply with the turn of a page
Adventures unfold, treasures untold
Await those who venture within
A book will take you to
Places you've never before been
Places you never imagined you'd go
Places unseen as if in a dream
Places better than the place you're in
So walk away from that rerun TV
Put down those dominoes
Leave the fussin' and the cussin' behind
Travel to new worlds, new adventures
Make new friends, set yourself free
Even if only temporarily
Your body may be bound
Within walls that surround
Yet the mind remains free
If one has a book to read
It's the best solution for life
While life is passing you by

Bro Kwesi | Thoughts

Inspirational thoughts
Running around in my mind

Trying to figure out
Which direction I should take

The trepidation I'm facing
Leaves me in a state of stagnation

Procrastinating

Motivation, dedication, and a
Persistent way of thinking

Are the only things going to
Help me reach my destination

Leaning towards liberation

       Will I make it?

David Snyder | Why I Write

I write because I have to -
to see the mundane pen and paper transcend
their physicality and become something
More.

I need to connect with
those receptive souls who can
tolerate me.

I write so that you
will help me die well.

Mayhap along the way a seed will be
planted, fostering.

I write because I am cloistered
with limited access to other souls.

To put into tangible form the beat
of this heart pained,

The breath drawn to move
me into our future

When we dance with joy
and wild abandon in the Rain.

I write because the words need
to be read, thumb their nose at

"nothing new under the sun."

I write to return to the glory of Her.

I write because you allow me the
privilege.

The spirits of our ancestors
dwell within us.

I write because I cannot contain it all.

the fire goes out
the flame of once-was
ceases to be
did she die
or is she merely at rest?
unbound from the need to consume,
no longer fettered
diffused throughout the cosmos
that which once seemed to be
never truly was
what had once possibly been
the alpha
has become transformed, convoluted,
doubled over onto itself
the nexus reached and passed,
consensual reality narrowed down,
the fulcrum
reaching a possible omega state
revealing that all, to the wise
noumenon and phenomenon
lose contrived substance
the two, where it may matter, become
interchangeable, unified in separation
made glorious for achieving
the state of nothingness, embers
of the mind, neither burning nor sleeping
a creation unto itself
self-fulfilling prophecy
which neither brings nor takes
joy nor misery

David Snyder | Untitled

moments do occur
much to my surprise
when the doors to cages
are shut
when the sun has set
and joy has fled
or our notion of it
anyhow
when the animals
that we made of ourselves
become still
become silent
quite possibly mindful
if not of anything seemingly
tangible
real
the breath remains.

Part 6

we make change happen /
beginning as we join
hands.

Eric Perez | To the Brave
                (A Poem Inspired by Ukraine)

To the lost ones, the fallen ones
To the ones who were lost
On the fields of grain and snow.
The ones who would not yield
Beneath the heel of the unjust ones.

I fear you - I do not have your courage,
Your strength, your will to rage
Against the tyrants, the oppressors.
To stand against the fright
Of their overwhelming might.

Oh my brothers, my sisters
How I pray to meet
The courage of your unyielding feet,
To stand my ground.
To pay the reaper's pound
So others may stand free.

Mocha | The Uvalde Children's Hearts Cry Silently

The Uvalde children's hearts cry silently,
but their suffering is written on their
         faces.
They hurt, they dream, they die violently
on our watch, out in the open-hidden
         places.
Victims of a world gone mad, victims of
         violence;
but turn the page and suddenly it's gone,
as they die quietly, as they suffer in
         silence.

These children live to die, never knowing
what hit them - we call it Life, they
never gave it a name.

They never saw the snake of fate that
bit them, but they lay slumped in the
saddle of its rattle just the same.

These children will succumb, in lonely
anguish they will die -

With their one burning question still
unanswered: why?

                These children's hearts
                Cry silently, never knowing
                Why they die violently

Turn the page - hurry, hurry, turn the
page

56

And return my attention to the
      all-important
Coffee pot, and things of such earthshaking
Earthquaking magnitude - needs another
      pack of sweetener
It's three degrees too hot. If I can't see
their faces, they're out of my mind.

Should I buy the the flower print laces, or
the designer one-of-a-kind? Priorities,
priorities, your rat in the race swallowed
down another day, but hey!

Another page turned, another thousand
children spurned, who made it to their
unmarked graves, thrown away...

            As their hearts cried
            ever silently, never knowing
            why they died violently

            It's still written
            on their faces,
            in those silent, dark places...

                        Turn the page.

Skye | Real Fake Individuals (excerpt)

People are going to be people, whether you
like it or not

Whether you like them or not

Whether they fit into your invisible world
or not

Is life as real as it ought to be? Or is
it perfunctory?

Are you as real as you ought to be? Or is
it perfunctory?

Let's put aside the defense and be honest.

We all seem to notice phoniness in every
individual.

Maybe because we're phony too!

Are you afraid to admit the truth to you?

Gary Farlow | Teamwork

In spite of resistance from our differences
and pockets of in-fighting, harsh words
we link arms in kinship
stitched together as one
in a life-force called courage
we kick off a journey as a unit
we stand as one.

In unity is strength
difference forgotten
we make change happen
beginning as we join hands.

To never allow "their" ignorance of
history define me as a man

To push against defeat, making a way for
my fam

Knowing where I come from, slavery in
which I was conceived

I know to work hard, never to beg on my
knees

I will wake every morrow in search of
liberation

From the drug and disease epidemic turning
a nation into patients

The song I sing: Sam Cooke's "Change Gonna
Come"

However long it takes to feel the impacts
of a generational curse

I stand out against its torment by
creating community

Like joining A.B.O. Comix, it takes a
village to raise a child

At times though, we need a democracy to
change minds

I vote for a better outcome

I scream mercy to police brutality and
injustices

All lives does matter but not unless
minority is included

I pray and pray against darkness that's
swallowing lives

As a beast of starvation does

What drives me is truth of history untold

Becoming entwined with causes and effects,
knowing this pandemic was like that

Why is it that "they" kill us with hate
but through love is our revenge of fighting
back?

Only love can conquer hate, no debate

To rise above negligence, to unchain the
chained

Open brains and fulfill my purpose, one
person at a time

What moves me is fighting back against the
setup and not falling victim to the odds

Against us, my brothers and sisters

We stand up against the great fall of
America.

Peace be unto you.

62

day is gone and night

is almost here

another broken heart filled with pain,

no more complaining

not shedding any more tears,

building up an army

with strong individuals

willing to stand united,

putting away differences

fighting hate, greed, corruption

standing for fallen soldiers

rise up, let's fight

tear these walls down

full of corruption

stand tall, never give up

make a difference

Afterword

This anthology resisted actualization.

Like the butterfly in its pupal stage, this collection of poems deals in the goo; vulnerable and squishy and steeped in possibility, this collection of writings by queer and trans incarcerated poets is caught in the moments just before resolution into a thing.

It is my privilege to muck about with our flutter of poets each year. This time around, I've been especially grateful to build an assemblage of poems that, while composed entirely of fully-realized works, comes together to leave the reader with a feeling of unfinished business.

HELP ME DIE WELL is a plea to loved ones, to circumstance - really, to everything - to make one's life worth living. To make sure the to-do list never runs out. To find the honor in the goo. Thanks to Gary Farlow for the title.

If you're reading this from inside and want to contribute to the next anthology, please write to:

    A.B.O. Comix c/o Poetry Anthology
    P.O. Box 11584
    195 41st St
    Oakland, CA 94611

I can't wait to hear from you.

- Ollie Mills

How to Help

Thank for reading these poems by incarcerat-
ed queer and trans writers. We hope they have
inspired you to take action on
behalf of the poets to work towards a
kinder, more compassionate world.

If you believe in our mission, you can help
support us by:

Donating or providing resources:
Venmo @abocomix | patreon.com/abocomix

Spreading the word and following our updates:
Instagram: @a.b.o.comix

Volunteering with us or hosting a fundraising
event: email abocomix@gmail.com

Writing to someone on the inside:
Go to www.abocomix.com/bios to get connected!

Talking to friends, family, neighbors, and
community members. Open up a dialogue and
remember to meet people where they're at.
Don't be afraid of difficult conversations and
do your best to maintain an open mind. You
may learn something.
When we know better, we can do better.

Starting your own creative project!
Against all odds, we're still here.
Still creating, still building friendships,
still optimistic about what we can achieve
when we work together. Take a chance, work
hard and you will do amazing things.
Trust us, we've been there.
Love and solidarity always!

9 781961 682023